The MAILBOX®

The Education Center®

MW00804265

Cut, Tear & Fold

Fine-Motor Skills for Little Learners

Fun activities and practice pages for increasing the following fine-motor skills:

- Strength
- Dexterity
- Control
- Coordination
  And more!

Over **85** ways to develop fine-motor skills!

Managing Editor: Sharon Murphy

Editorial Team: Becky S. Andrews, Kimberley Bruck, Diane Badden, Thad H. McLaurin, Lynn Drolet, Kelly Robertson, Karen A. Brudnak, Juli Docimo Blair, Hope Rodgers, Dorothy C. McKinney, Janet Boyce, Catherine Broome-Kehm, Lucia Kemp Henry, Leanne Swinson, Carole Watkins

Production Team: Lori Z. Henry, Pam Crane, Rebecca Saunders, Chris Curry, Sarah Foreman, Theresa Lewis Goode, Greg D. Rieves, Eliseo De Jesus Santos II, Barry Slate, Donna K. Teal, Zane Williard, Tazmen Carlisle, Kathy Coop, Marsha Heim, Lynette Dickerson, Mark Rainey

www.themailbox.com

Printed in the United States
10 9 8 7 6 5 4 3 2

HPS221332

Table of Contents

Why Practice Fine-Motor Skills?

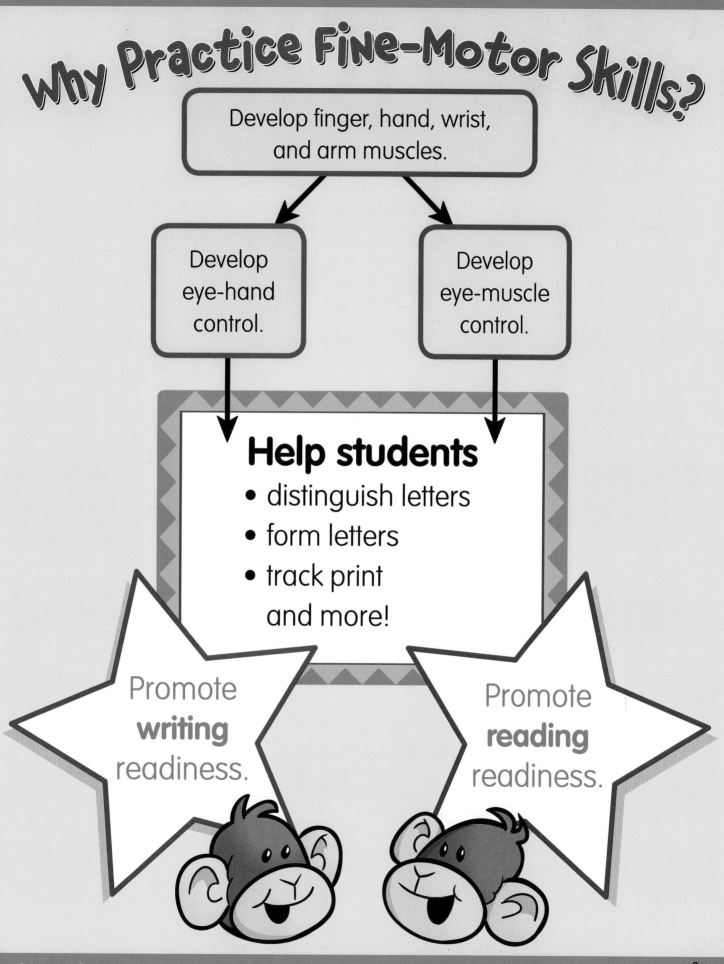

Develop finger, hand, wrist, and arm muscles.

Develop eye-hand control.

Develop eye-muscle control.

Help students
- distinguish letters
- form letters
- track print and more!

Promote **writing** readiness.

Promote **reading** readiness.

CUT

Sunny Skies

Materials
- yellow strip of triangles (patterns on page 19)
- construction paper
  —6" circle of yellow
  —9" x 12" sheet of blue
- crayons
- glue
- scissors

To make a sun, a student draws a face on the yellow circle and glues it onto his blue paper. Then he cuts the yellow paper strip into triangles and glues one edge of each cutout to the circle to make the sun's rays. After the glue dries, he carefully curls the point of each ray for a "sun-sational" 3-D effect.

Humpty Dumpty's Wall

Materials
- Humpty Dumpty cutout (patterns on page 20)
- construction paper
  —two 1" x 9" strips of red
  —9" x 12" sheet of any color
- scissors
- glue
- crayons

To make bricks for Humpty Dumpty's wall, a child cuts the red strips into smaller pieces. Next, she glues the bricks onto her paper to make a wall. After she colors the Humpty Dumpty cutout to her liking, she glues it to the top of the wall.

Individual   Confetti Cutting

To begin her project, a youngster colors a hat cutout and glues it to the white paper. Then she cuts the paper strips into smaller pieces and glues the resulting confetti around the hat. For an added touch, she glues the pom-pom to the top of the hat.

Materials
- party hat cutout (pattern on page 21)
- construction paper
  — 9" x 12" sheet of white
  — ½" x 9" strips of various colors
- crayons
- glue
- scissors
- pom-pom

Individual   "Hand-y" Memorabilia

To make a keepsake, a child lays his hands, palms down, on the half sheet of paper. Use a marker to trace the child's hands. Then the youngster carefully cuts around each handprint and glues the cutouts onto the black paper. To complete the keepsake, use the white crayon to write the child's name and age and the date on the project.

Kevin - Age 4

September 1, 2007

Materials
- construction paper
  —4½" x 6" sheet of any color
  —9" x 12" sheet of black
- thick marker
- scissors
- glue
- white crayon

Comfy Nest

Materials
- hen cutout
  (patterns on page 22)
- construction paper
  —9" x 12" sheet
  —scraps of yellow
- scissors
- glue
- crayons

To make a nest, a student cuts the yellow scraps into smaller strips that resemble hay. Then she glues the hay to her paper to create a nest. Finally, she colors the hen cutout and glues it onto the nest.

Newsworthy Cutting

Materials
- newspaper
- tape
- scissors
- marker

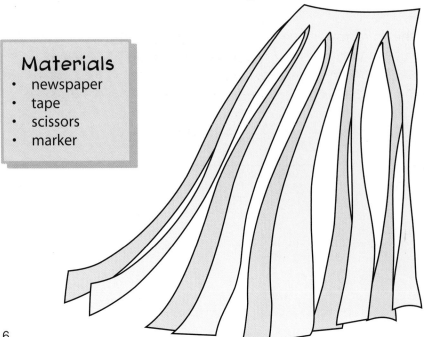

To prepare this center, draw thick cutting lines on individual sheets of newspaper to create thin vertical strips. Then, for each center visitor, tape the top of a prepared sheet to the edge of a table. To begin, a youngster sits on the floor and cuts the newspaper along the lines from the bottom to the top. The resulting fringe creates a perfect passageway for him to crawl under the table to get a new view of the room! If desired, place picture books under the table for children to look at.

CUT

Center · Bread Cubes

When a child visits the center, she places a slice of bread on a plate. Then she uses the knife to cut the bread into long strips. Next, she cuts each strip into cubes and places the cubes in the bowl. After each youngster has visited the center, lead the class outside to feed the birds the resulting bread cubes.

Materials
- slice of day-old bread
- large paper plate
- plastic knife
- large plastic bowl

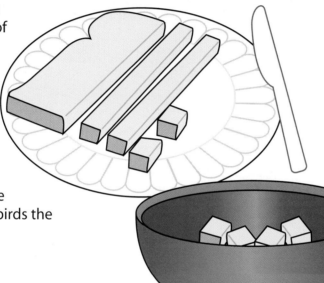

Individual · Scarecrow Bag

These scarecrow bags are perfect for holding festive fall treats! To make one, a youngster colors the scarecrow cutout's face and glues it to the front of the bag at the bottom. While the bag is still closed, he cuts strips from the top of the bag to the face. (If desired, program each bag with cutting lines.) After opening the bag, he folds down the cut strips to create the scarecrow's hair. Then he trims the strips above the scarecrow's face to create bangs (with assistance). To complete the project, staple the yellow strip to the bag to make a handle.

Materials
- scarecrow face cutout (patterns on page 23)
- construction paper —1" x 12" strip of yellow
- paper lunch bag
- crayons
- glue
- scissors
- stapler

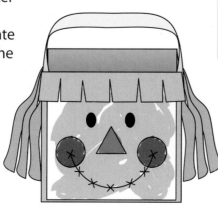

Snips of Straws

Materials
- coffee-stirring straws
- wide plastic container
- scissors

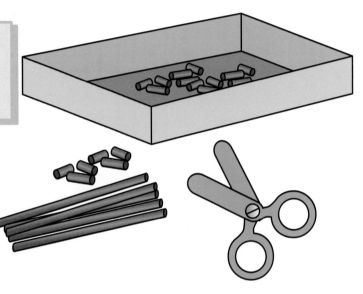

When a child visits the center, she cuts the straws into small pieces. As she cuts, she aims to snip each piece into the container. Before she leaves the area, she empties the container at a designated location. Save the snips for future use at a sensory table or for making collages.

Magazine Meals

Materials
- magazines
- 9" paper plate
- scissors
- glue

To make a meal, a youngster looks through the magazines to find pictures of food. He cuts out the pictures and glues them to the paper plate. If desired, showcase the completed projects on a table for all to see.

CUT

Whole Group
Fringed Feathers

To prepare, post a simple featherless turkey cutout on a bulletin board or wall. Have each student carefully cut on the lines of a feather cutout. Then help him attach his fringed feather to the turkey.

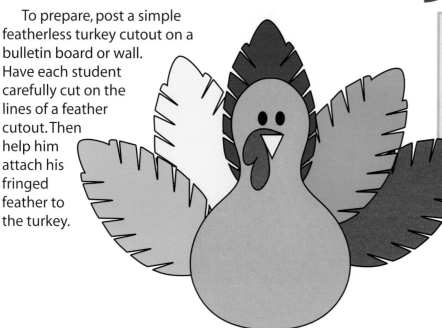

Materials
- feather cutouts of various colors (pattern on page 24)
- turkey cutout
- scissors
- stapler or tape

Center
Cookie Cutting

When a child visits the center, he uses the rolling pin to create a smooth layer of play dough. Then he lays a shape template on the dough and uses the knife to cut around the shape. He places the resulting cookie on the cookie sheet and continues in this manner until he has created several cookies. Finally, he removes the cookies from the cookie sheet and rolls them into a ball of dough for the next center visitor.

Materials
- circle, square, and triangle foam templates
- play dough
- small rolling pin
- plastic knife
- cookie sheet

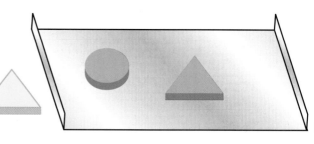

How Sweet!

Materials
- candy cane cutout (pattern on page 25)
- construction paper —1¾" x 12" strip of red
- scissors
- glue

To make stripes for the candy cane, a student snips the red strip into rectangular pieces. Then he glues the resulting stripes onto his candy cane cutout. If desired, display the completed projects around the door for a sweet welcome!

Tree Trimming Whole Group

Materials
- construction paper —9" x 12" sheets of green (programmed as shown)
- scissors
- stapler or tape

For this class-made tree, each youngster cuts on the programmed lines of a green sheet of paper. Display the cut papers so that they resemble a tree. If desired, embellish the tree with student-made ornaments and a glittery star.

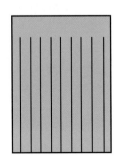

10

CUT

Individual

Simply Snow

To make a snowflake scene, a youngster cuts her strip into thin rectangles. Then she arranges the rectangles to resemble snowflakes and glues them to her paper. If desired, use the completed papers to create a snowy background for a seasonal display.

Materials
- construction paper
  —4" x 9" strip of white
  —9" x 12" sheet of blue
- scissors
- glue

Individual

Penguin's Igloo

To begin her project, a youngster colors the penguin cutout and glues it to the blue paper. Then she cuts the white paper so that the pieces resemble blocks of ice. To complete the project, the child glues the blocks around the penguin to create an igloo.

Materials
- penguin cutout (patterns on page 26)
- construction paper
  —9" x 12" sheet of blue
  —1" x 9" strips of white
- crayons
- scissors
- glue

Alphabet Soup

Materials
- magazines
- construction paper
  —6" circle of red
- 9" paper plate
- glue
- scissors
- plastic spoon

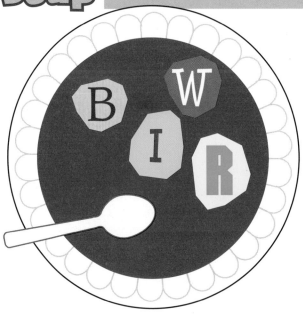

To make alphabet soup, a student glues the red circle to his paper plate. Then he searches through a magazine for letters of the alphabet. He cuts out desired letters and glues them to the red circle. To complete the project, he glues the spoon to the plate.

Spiral Snake

Materials
- snake cutout (pattern on page 27)
- scissors

To make a snake, a student cuts along the thick line, beginning at the dot and ending at the head. If desired, encourage youngsters to color their snakes. *Ssss…*

CUT

Individual

Hairy Cut Ups

To begin his project, a youngster colors the outer half circle (hair) and draws a face in the center of the plate. Then he cuts on the thick lines to create hair.

Materials
- large paper plate (prepared as shown)
- crayons
- scissors

Individual

Personal Pizza

To make a pizza, a student cuts the paper scraps to create toppings and cuts the yarn lengths into shorter pieces for shredded cheese. Next, she fingerpaints her circle so that the paint resembles sauce. While the paint is wet, she arranges the toppings on the sauce and sprinkles the cheese on top. Then she gently presses the ingredients into the sauce and sets the pizza aside to dry. If desired, display the pizzas on a red-and-white checkered background. Yum!

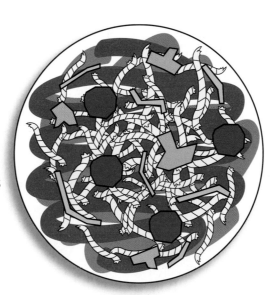

Materials
- construction paper —scraps of various colors
- yellow yarn lengths
- 9" tagboard circle
- scissors
- red fingerpaint

13

Lion's Mane

Materials
- brown lion face cutout (pattern on page 28)
- construction paper —12" circle of yellow
- glue
- scissors

To make a lion, a student glues the lion face in the middle of his yellow circle. He fringe-cuts the circle so that it resembles a lion's mane. Then he gently scrunches the resulting strips for a "grrrreat" finish!

Whimsical Windsock

Materials
- construction paper —9" x 12" sheet of white
- five 9" crepe paper strips
- scissors
- tape
- hole puncher
- 12" yarn length

To make a windsock, a youngster colors one side of the white paper with seasonal or other desired details. Then she flips her paper over and glues one end of each crepe paper strip along the bottom of her paper. When the glue dries, she cuts each strip to create thinner streamers. (If needed, secure the paper for easier cutting.) Next, she rolls the paper so the edges meet, keeping her design on the outside, and tapes it closed (with assistance). To prepare the windsock for hanging, punch two holes near the top of the cylinder on opposite sides of the project. Then thread each end of the yarn through the holes and make knots.

CUT

Funny Faces

Individual

To make a unique face, a student looks through the magazines to find two eyes, a nose, and a mouth. He cuts out the facial features, arranges them on his oval so they resemble a face, and glues them in place. Then he cuts magazine scraps into strips and glues them to the head to make hair.

Materials
- magazines
- construction paper —large oval
- scissors
- glue

More Sprinkles, Please!

Individual

To make a cupcake, a student colors the cupcake cutout to her liking. Then she cuts the paper strips to make sprinkles. Finally, she uses a paintbrush to spread glue on the frosting and scatters the sprinkles on top.

Materials
- cupcake cutout (pattern on page 29)
- construction paper —thin strips of various colors
- crayons
- scissors
- paintbrush
- diluted glue

15

Wiggle Wand

Materials
- construction paper —9" x 12" sheet
- five 9" crepe paper strips
- glue
- scissors
- tape

To make a wand, a student glues one end of each strip across the bottom of the paper. When the glue dries, she cuts up each crepe paper strip to create thinner streamers. (If needed, secure the paper to the table for easier cutting.) Then she holds her paper with the streamers hanging down, rolls the paper into a long tube, and tapes down the overlapping edge (with assistance). If desired, play a musical melody and encourage youngsters to wave their wiggle wands to the beat!

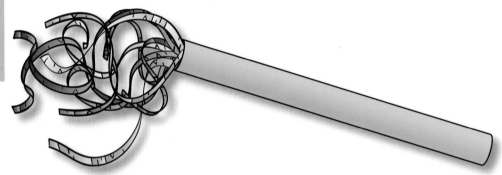

Slicing the Cake

Materials
- cake pan
- play dough
- plastic knife
- plastic plates
- spatula

Youngsters slice and serve cake at this fun center. To begin, a child covers the bottom of a cake pan with a layer of play dough. Then he uses the knife to carefully cut the resulting cake into slices. Once he has sliced the cake, he uses the spatula to place each cake serving on a separate plate. To prepare for the next center visitor, he rolls the dough into a ball and returns it to its container. If desired, place an apron at the center for your little bakers to wear.

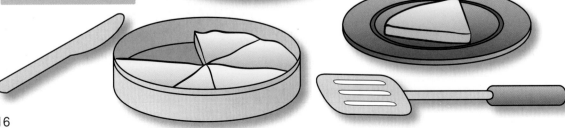

Individual — Lovely Lily Pad

To make the flower, a youngster cuts the ribbed outer edges of each cupcake liner as shown. He glues the small cupcake liner to the center of the larger liner and then glues the resulting flower atop the lily pad cutout. If desired, use the completed lily pads to embellish a pond-related display.

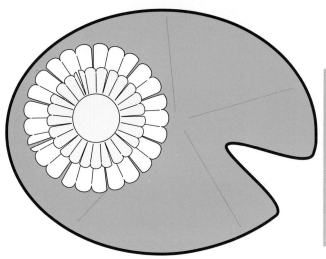

Materials
- green lily pad cutout (pattern on page 30)
- 2 different sizes of cupcake liners
- scissors
- glue

Individual — Beautiful Butterfly

To make a butterfly, a youngster colors the butterfly body on her cutout. She cuts the tissue paper into smaller pieces. Then she uses the paintbrush to apply a thin layer of glue to the wings and places the tissue paper pieces on the glue.

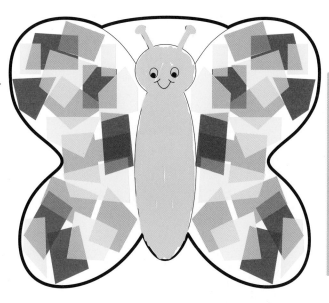

Materials
- butterfly cutout (pattern on page 31)
- crayons
- colorful tissue paper scraps
- scissors
- paintbrush
- diluted glue

Frilly Flower

Materials
- construction paper
  —1½" x 9" strip of green
  —2 leaf cutouts
- 9" paper plate
- crayons
- scissors
- glue

To make a flower, a student colors the plate to resemble a flower head. Then she fringe-cuts the plate's rim to create petals. Next, she glues the leaf cutouts to the paper strip (stem) and then glues one end of the stem to the flower head. Finally, she bends some of the petals forward to create a 3-D blossom.

Festive Fireworks

Materials
- construction paper
  —9" x 12" sheet of black
- ribbons of various colors
- scissors
- glue
- star stickers

To make a firework, a youngster cuts the ribbons into smaller pieces. Then he squeezes glue in arching bands (with assistance) to resemble a bursting firework. He sprinkles the cut ribbons over the glue and gently shakes off the excess. When the glue is dry, he embellishes his project with star stickers.

Check out the fine-motor reproducibles on pages 32–37.

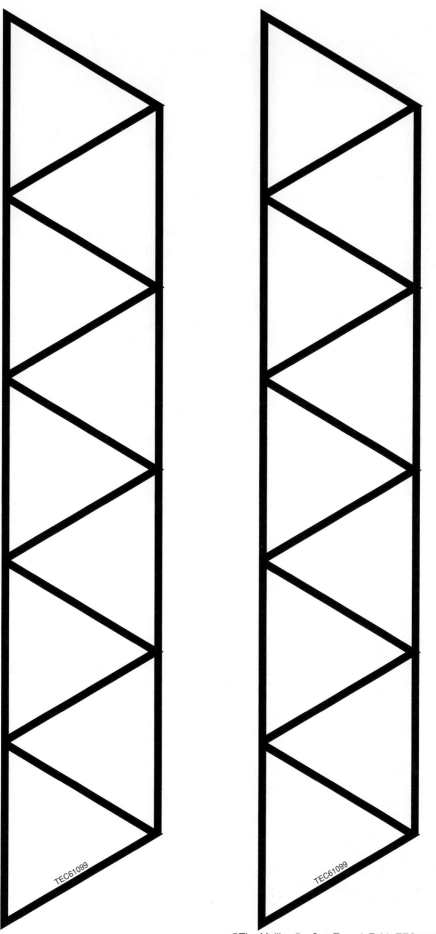

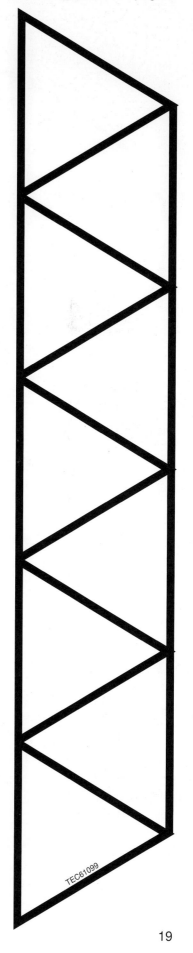

TEC61099

TEC61099

TEC61099

©The Mailbox® • *Cut, Tear, & Fold* • TEC61099

Humpty Dumpty Patterns
Use with "Humpty Dumpty's Wall" on page 4.

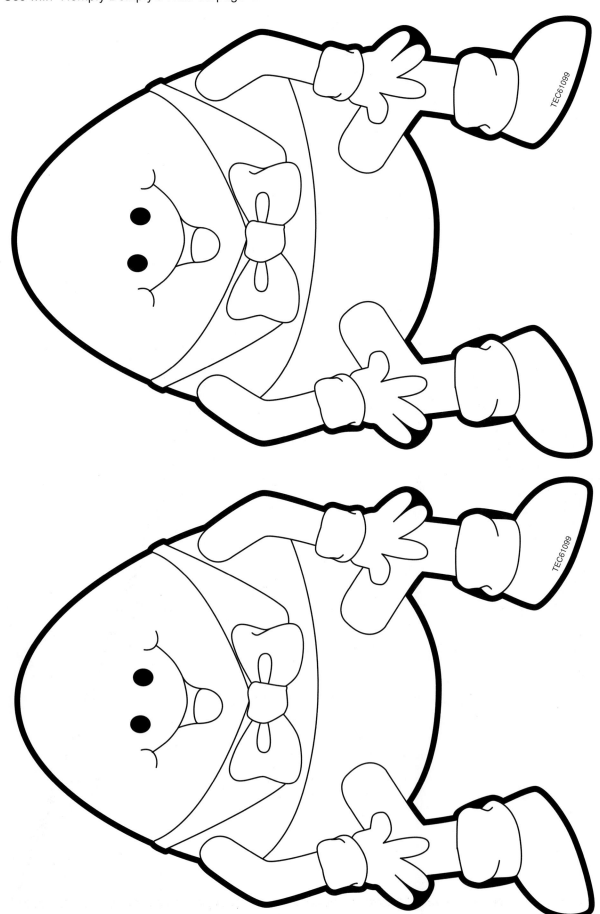

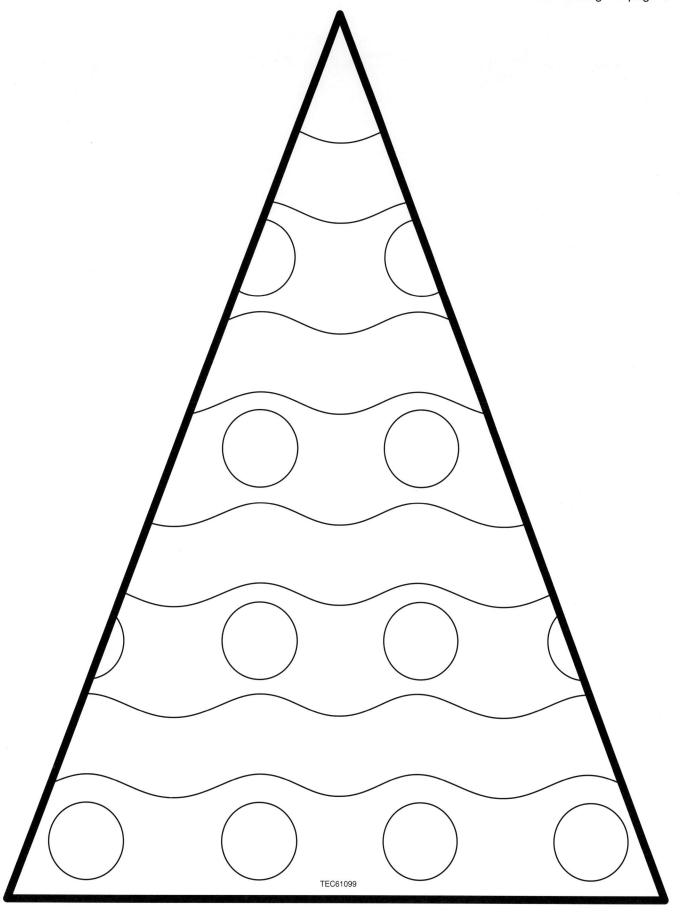

TEC61099

Hen Patterns
Use with "Comfy Nest" on page 6.

TEC61099

TEC61099

TEC61099

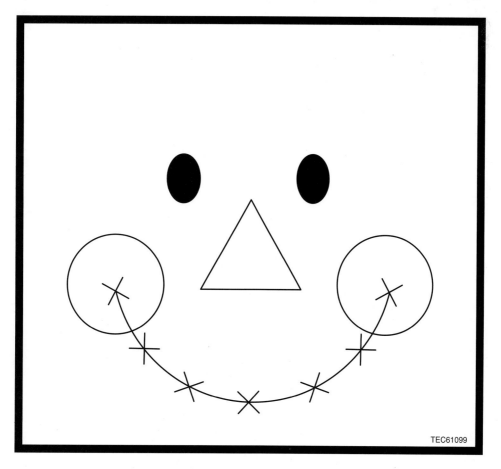

TEC61099

Feather Pattern
Use with "Fringed Feathers" on page 9.

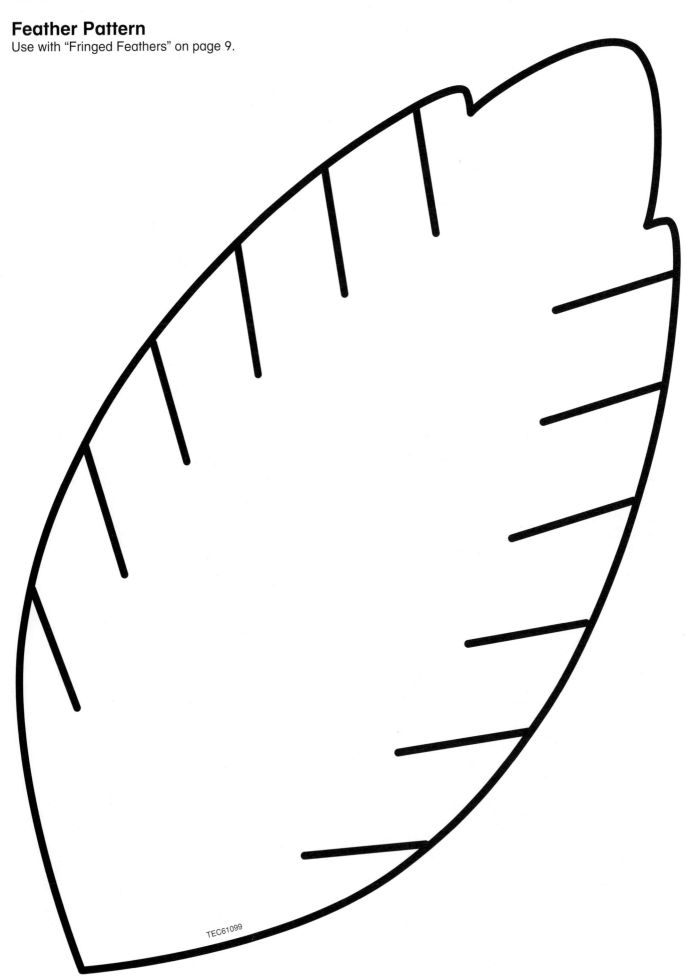

TEC61099

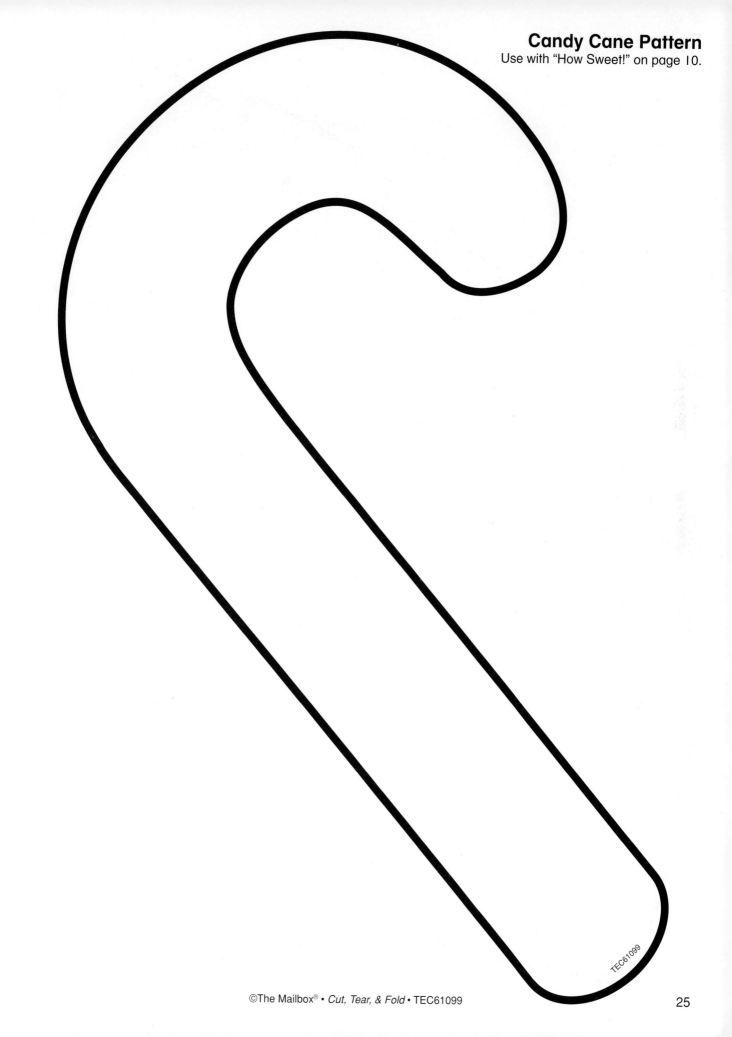

Candy Cane Pattern
Use with "How Sweet!" on page 10.

TEC61099

Penguin Patterns
Use with "Penguin's Igloo" on page 11.

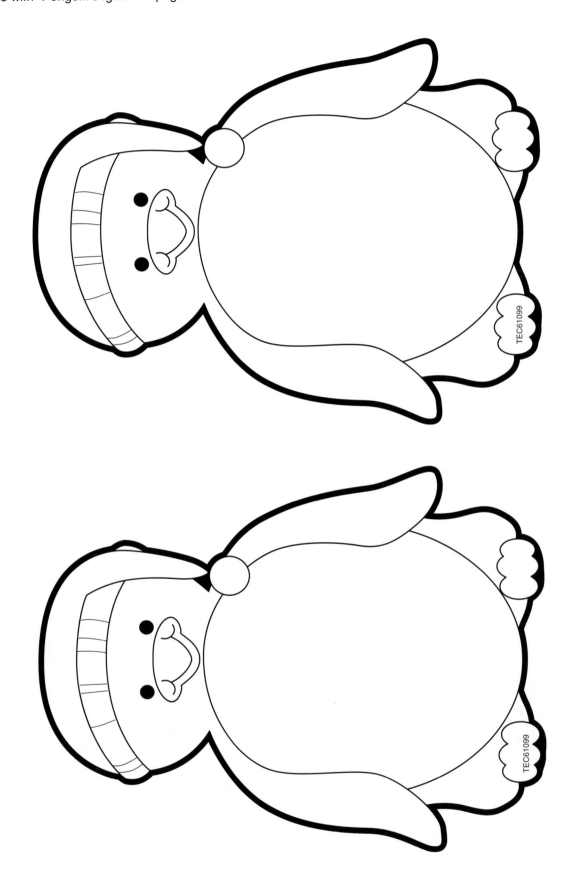

TEC61099

TEC61099

TEC61099

Lion Face Pattern
Use with "Lion's Mane" on page 14.

TEC61099

TEC61099

Lily Pad Pattern
Use with "Lovely Lily Pad" on page 17.

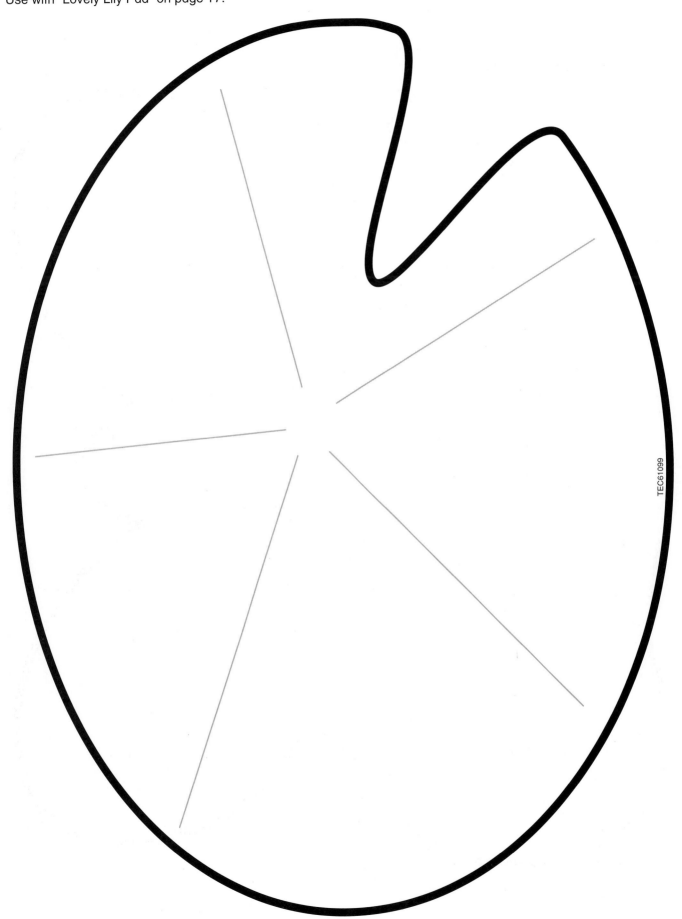

TEC61099

Name _____

High Flying

Cut.

Name _____

Clown's Haircut

Color.

Cut.

Name _____

Ice Hockey

Cut.

Glue.

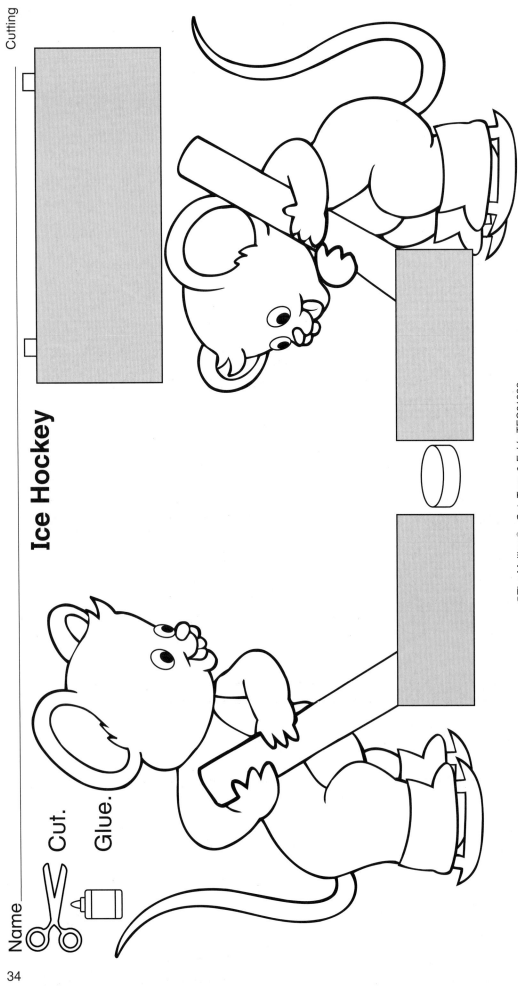

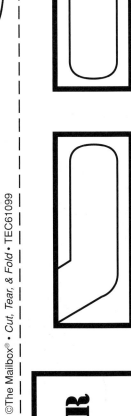

HOME **VISITOR**

3 **3**

©The Mailbox® • *Cut, Tear, & Fold* • TEC61099

Pizza Pup

✂ Cut.

🧴 Glue.

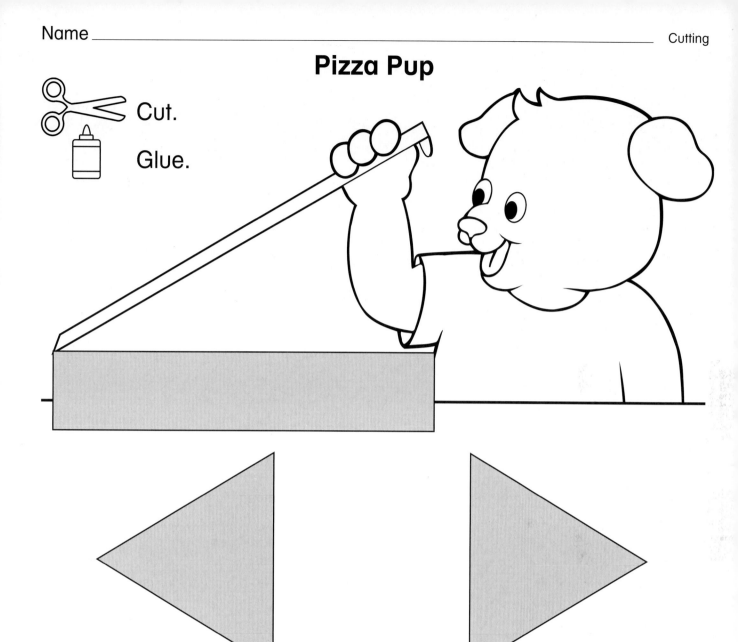

Pizza

35

Munching Lunch

✂ Cut.

Glue.

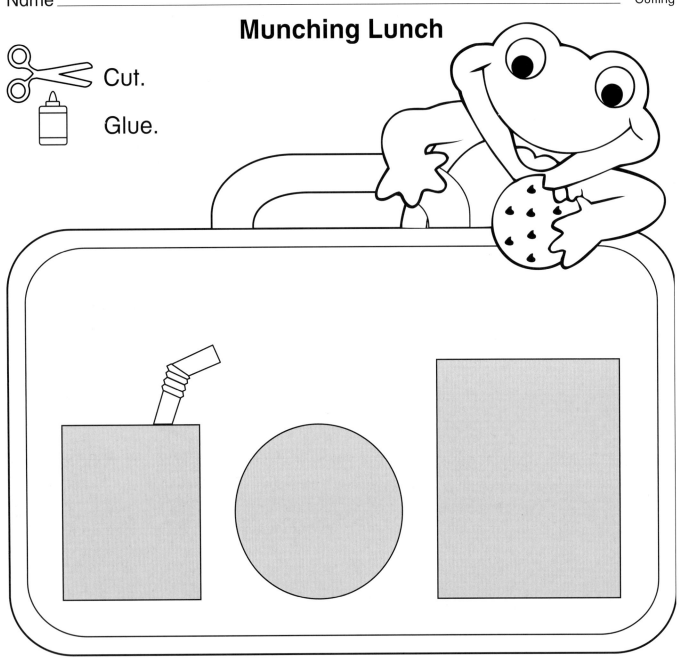

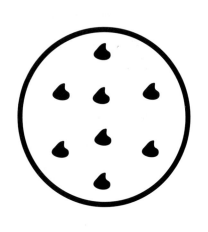

Milk

Home, Tweet Home!

Name

Cut.

Glue.

37

TEAR

A Welcome Display

For this class-made display, title the bulletin board paper "Welcome." Then use the markers to draw an outline of a large apple with a stem and a leaf as shown. Have youngsters tear the construction paper scraps into small pieces and glue them in the corresponding sections of the apple. Showcase the artwork outside your classroom door.

Materials
- construction paper —scraps of red, green, and brown
- bulletin board paper
- red, green, and brown markers
- glue

Welcome!

Gobs of Grass
Center

When a child visits the center, he tears paper scraps and crepe paper into small pieces to resemble grass and places them in the tub. When the tub is partially filled, help him pour the contents into your sensory table. After everyone has contributed paper grass to the table, prepare another fine-motor workout by mixing in an assortment of plastic bugs or the bug cutouts. Have students find and remove the bugs with a pair of tweezers or tongs.

Materials
- plastic bugs or bug cutouts (patterns on page 52)
- construction paper —scraps of green
- small tub
- green crepe paper
- plastic tweezers or tongs

38

Individual

Suncatcher

To make a suncatcher, a student tears tissue paper scraps into smaller pieces. When she has a supply of torn paper, lay one square of Con-Tact covering sticky-side up on her work surface. The student arranges the tissue paper pieces on the covering to her liking. Seal her work with the second square of Con-Tact covering and trim any sticky edges. Then hole-punch her project, thread a length of yarn through the hole, and knot the ends. For a sun-catching display, suspend the projects in a sunny site.

Materials
- clear Con-Tact covering —two 9" squares
- colorful tissue paper scraps
- scissors
- hole puncher
- yarn

Center

Hidden Nuts

Youngsters pretend to be squirrels when they visit this center. Place the bag of leaves and the pom-poms near your sensory table. A child tears a handful of leaves or leaf cutouts into small pieces to create a leafy pile. Then he pretends that he is a squirrel preparing for winter and hides the brown pom-poms (nuts) in the pile. To ready the center for the next visitor, he removes the pom-poms and torn leaves from the table.

Materials
- bag of leaves or leaf cutouts
- brown pom-poms

Furry Teddy Bear

Materials
- brown bear face cutout (patterns on page 53)
- construction paper —scraps of brown
- small paper plate
- glue
- black marker

To make a bear, a child tears the construction paper scraps into smaller pieces and glues them in an overlapping fashion to an inverted paper plate. Then he glues the bear face cutout on the resulting fur as shown. Next, he tears two ear shapes and glues them to the plate. Finally, he uses the black marker to draw two eyes and ear details.

Pretty Placemat

Materials
- construction paper —9" x 12" sheet of white
- tissue paper
- wide paintbrush
- diluted glue
- scissors

Add a burst of color to snacktime with this unique placemat. To make one, a student tears tissue paper into strips. Then she uses a wide paintbrush to spread a thin layer of glue on the white paper. She lays the strips on the glue as desired. When the project is dry, trim any excess tissue paper from the edges and laminate the resulting placemat.

TEAR

Center
Neat Note

To make a note at this center, a student tears a sheet of paper from the notebook. Then he tears away the ragged edges to make a neat edge. To complete the note, he uses the crayons to write a message or draw a picture. If desired, encourage him to hand-deliver his note.

Materials
- spiral-bound notebook
- crayons

Individual
Indian Corn

To make an ear of corn, a youngster tears the photos or magazine pages into kernel-size pieces. She glues the pieces, in rows, to the corn cutout to resemble Indian corn. Then she tears the crepe paper into strips (husks) and glues the husks to her project as shown.

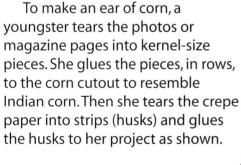

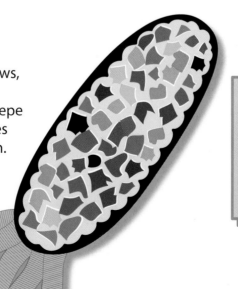

Materials
- yellow corn cutout (patterns on page 54)
- old photographs or magazines
- glue
- green crepe paper

Tape Tearing

To make a storage box, group members tear strips of masking tape and attach them in an overlapping fashion to the shoebox and its lid. Then they sponge-paint the box and lid and set them aside to dry. Use the box to store manipulatives, craft supplies, or scrap paper.

Materials
- shoebox
- masking tape
- sponges
- paint

Mosaic in the Making

Materials
- construction paper —9" x 12" sheet
- calendar or magazine picture
- glue

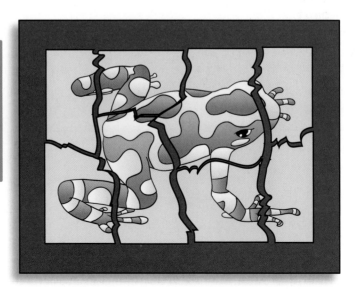

To make a mosaic, a student tears her picture into no more than ten pieces. She arranges the pieces on the paper (with assistance), leaving narrow spaces between them. Then she glues the pieces in place.

TEAR

Individual   Jaguar's Spots

To make a spotted jaguar, a student tears black scraps into small pieces that resemble spots. He glues the spots to the jaguar cutout. Then he tears the brown scraps into smaller spots and glues them atop the black spots.

Materials
- orange jaguar cutout (pattern on page 55)
- construction paper —scraps of black and brown
- glue

Individual   Treasure Map

In preparation for this project, cut the bottom panel from the bag and discard it. Cut the remaining bag in half and give one piece to the student. (Save the remaining paper bag piece for another child.)

To make a map, a youngster tears away the edges of the bag piece. Next, she repeatedly crumples and opens the bag piece to give the map a worn appearance. Then she uses crayons to add map details, such as trees, lakes, and an X to mark the spot of a buried treasure.

Materials
- large brown paper bag
- crayons

Let It Snow!

To create a snowfall at this center, a youngster tears the paper scraps into small pieces (snowflakes). After creating a small mound, he shovels the snow into the bucket.

Materials
- white paper scraps
- small plastic shovel
- bucket

Shiny Smiles

To begin this project, a student tears the aluminum foil into small pieces. Then she arranges the pieces on the paper to make a smiley face and glues them in place.

Materials
- construction paper —9" x 12" sheet
- aluminum foil
- glue

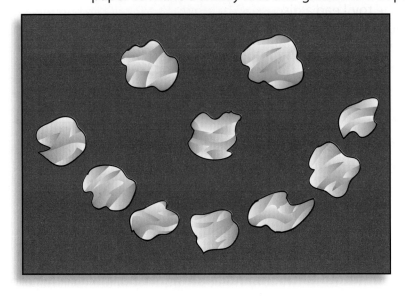

TEAR

Individual   Snowpal

To make a snowpal, a youngster glues the circles onto the blue paper as shown. He tears the paper scraps to create facial details and glues them on the top circle. Then he tears additional scraps to embellish his snowpal with items such as a hat, a broom, and buttons.

Materials
- construction paper
  —two 6" circles of white
  —12" x 18" sheet of blue
  —scraps of various colors
- glue

Whole Group   Toy Box

To create a toy box, students tear pictures of toys from magazines or catalogs and place them in a box labeled as shown. Then, for a fun follow-up, invite a youngster to remove a picture and name the toy. Lead a discussion on how the toy might be used individually, with a friend, or with a group. Continue in this manner, as time permits, with more pictures.

Materials
- magazines or catalogs
- shoebox

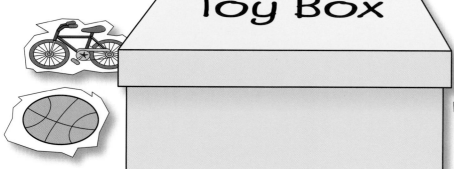

Nicely Nestled Eggs

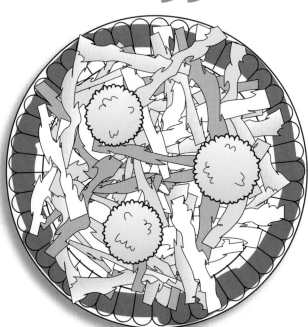

Materials
- construction paper —scraps of yellow
- newspaper
- brown lunch bag
- paper towel
- small paper bowl
- brown crayon
- three 1" pom-poms

To make a nest, a child colors the bowl's rim with the brown crayon. Then she tears the yellow paper scraps, newspaper, bag, and paper towel into thin strips and layers them in the bowl. To complete her project, she nestles three pom-poms (eggs) into the resulting nest.

Tickets, Please!

Materials
- roll of tickets

This class activity is the ticket to improving youngsters' fine-motor and counting skills. To begin, give a student volunteer the roll of tickets. Announce a number and lead the class in slowly counting aloud to that number while the child tears off the corresponding number of tickets. Continue in this manner until each child has had a turn. For an added challenge, have each student tear his torn tickets into smaller pieces.

TEAR

Center
Salad Snack

Even the littlest hands can tear lettuce leaves! After washing her hands, a youngster peels a leaf from the head of lettuce at the center. Then she tears the leaf into several smaller pieces and puts them in the bowl. She pours dressing over the leaves and enjoys her tasty snack!

Materials
- head of lettuce
- disposable bowls
- salad dressing
- plastic forks

Ranch Salad Dressing

Individual
"Moo-velous" Spots

To make the cow's spots, a child tears the paper scraps into small pieces and glues them to the cow cutout. If desired, give the completed cows a pasture to graze on by mounting them on a length of green bulletin board paper.

Materials
- cow cutout
  (pattern on page 56)
- construction paper
  — scraps of brown or black

Splish, Splash!

Materials
- 2 yellow duck cutouts (patterns on page 57)
- construction paper — 9" x 12" sheet of blue
- glue

To make a pond, a child tears the edges of the blue paper to create a large pond shape. Then he leads the duck cutouts to the pond to play. After a designated amount of playtime, he glues the ducks to the pond.

Radiant Rainbow

To prepare, use the marker to draw thick arches that resemble a rainbow. Then glue one piece of each tissue paper color in the corresponding rainbow arches. To complete the rainbow, youngsters tear the tissue paper into small pieces. Then they glue the pieces to the

Materials
- bulletin board paper
- tissue paper of rainbow colors
- marker
- glue

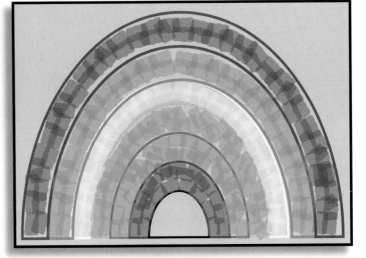

corresponding color arches on the rainbow. If desired, stretch out cotton balls and glue them on both ends of the rainbow. When the glue is dry, display the completed project for a burst of beautiful colors!

TEAR

Individual — Mouthwatering Melon

To make a watermelon slice, a student tears the green scraps into small pieces and glues them to the rounded edge of the semicircle to create a rind. Then she tears the black scraps to make watermelon seeds and glues them to the slice.

Materials
- construction paper
  —semicircle of red
  —scraps of green and black

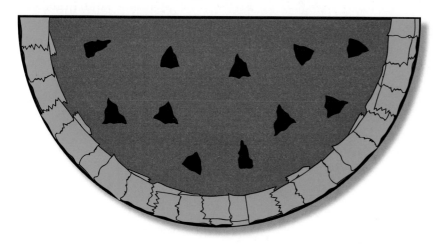

Center — Sticky Scales

To make a fish at this center, a student tears small pieces of masking tape and overlaps them on a fish cutout to make scales. He uses the crayons to color the scales as desired. Then he places a large sticky dot on the fish to make an eye.

Materials
- fish cutouts
  (patterns on page 58)
- masking tape
- glitter crayons
- large sticky dots

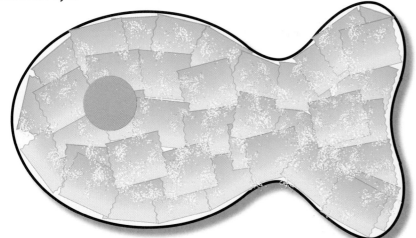

"Dino-mite" Tearing

Materials
- dinosaur cutout (pattern on page 59)
- construction paper —scraps of any color
- glue

To make a stegosaurus, a child tears the construction paper scraps into triangles to make scales. Then she glues the scales to the dinosaur cutout as shown. Now that's a "tear–ific" dinosaur!

Beach Ball Bonanza

Materials
- beach ball cutout (pattern on page 60)
- tissue paper of six different colors

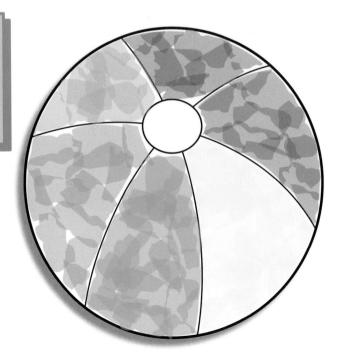

To make a beach ball, a student tears tissue paper of different colors into small pieces. Then he glues the pieces to his beach ball cutout, using one color for each section.

TEAR

Individual   Terrific Turtle

To make a turtle, a student tears the tissue paper into small pieces and glues the pieces to an inverted paper plate (shell). Then she glues the head, leg, and tail patterns (with assistance, if necessary) to the underside of the shell. If desired, arrange the turtles on a bulletin board for a 3-D display!

Materials
- brown turtle body part cutouts (patterns on page 61)
- green tissue paper
- glue
- 9" heavy-duty coated paper plate

Individual   Bag on the Go!

This decorative bag is perfect for toting items to and from school. To make one, a student tears the various paper supplies into small pieces and glues them to his bag in a desired design. When the bag is dry, help him write his name on his bag.

Materials
- construction paper —scraps of any color
- scrapbook paper scraps
- small gift bag
- glue
- wide marker

Check out the fine-motor reproducibles on pages 62–65.

51

Bug Patterns

Use with "Gobs of Grass" on page 38.

TEC61099

TEC61099

TEC61099

TEC61099

TEC61099

TEC61099

Corn Patterns
Use with "Indian Corn" on page 41.

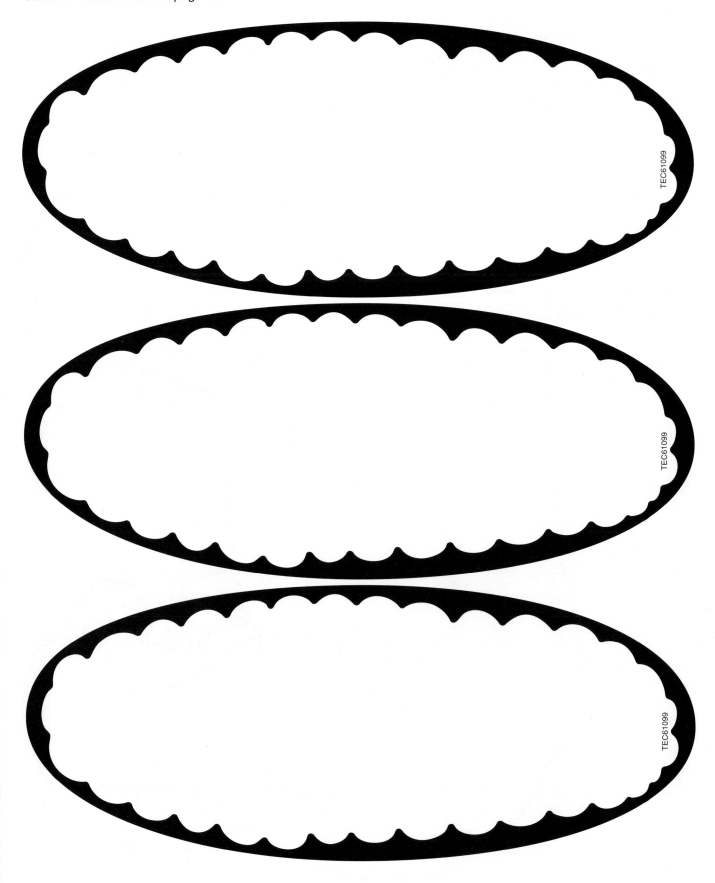

TEC61099

TEC61099

TEC61099

TEC61099

Cow Pattern
Use with "'Moo-velous' Spots" on page 47.

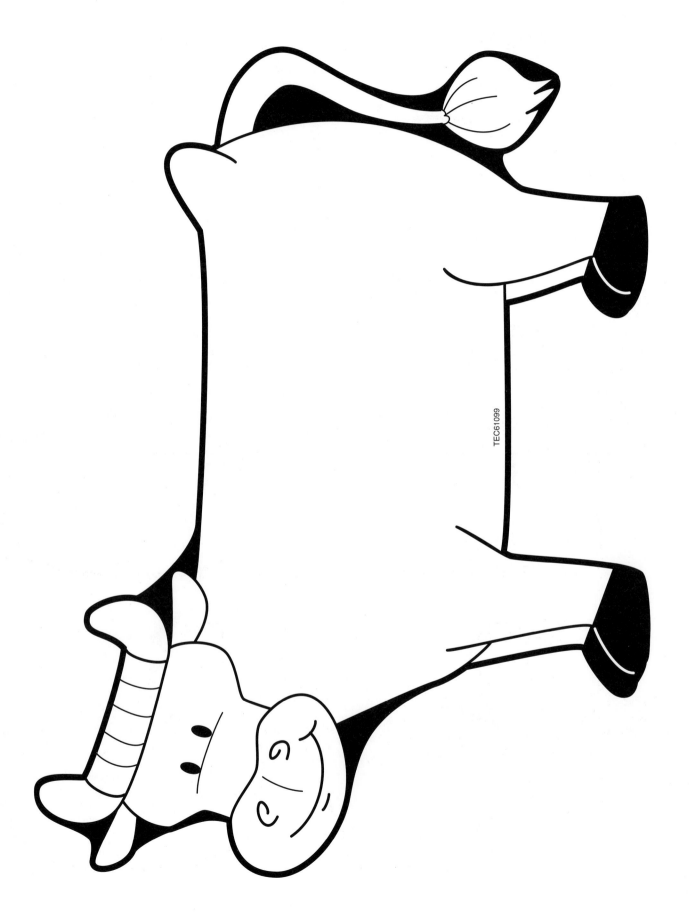

TEC61099

TEC61099

TEC61099

TEC61099

TEC61099

TEC61099

TEC61099

Fish Patterns

Use with "Sticky Scales" on page 49.

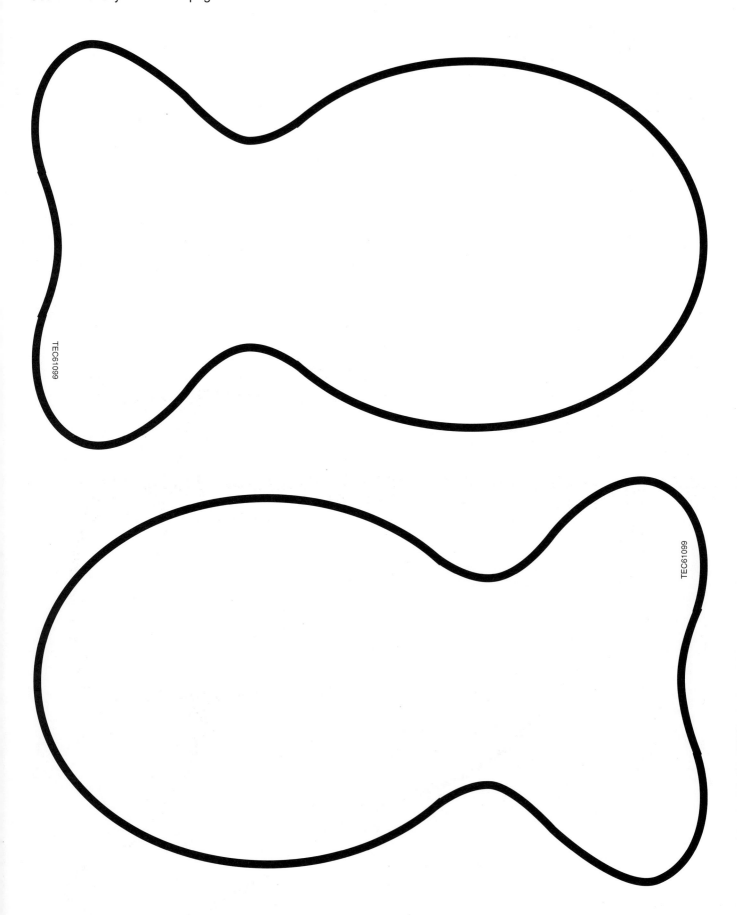

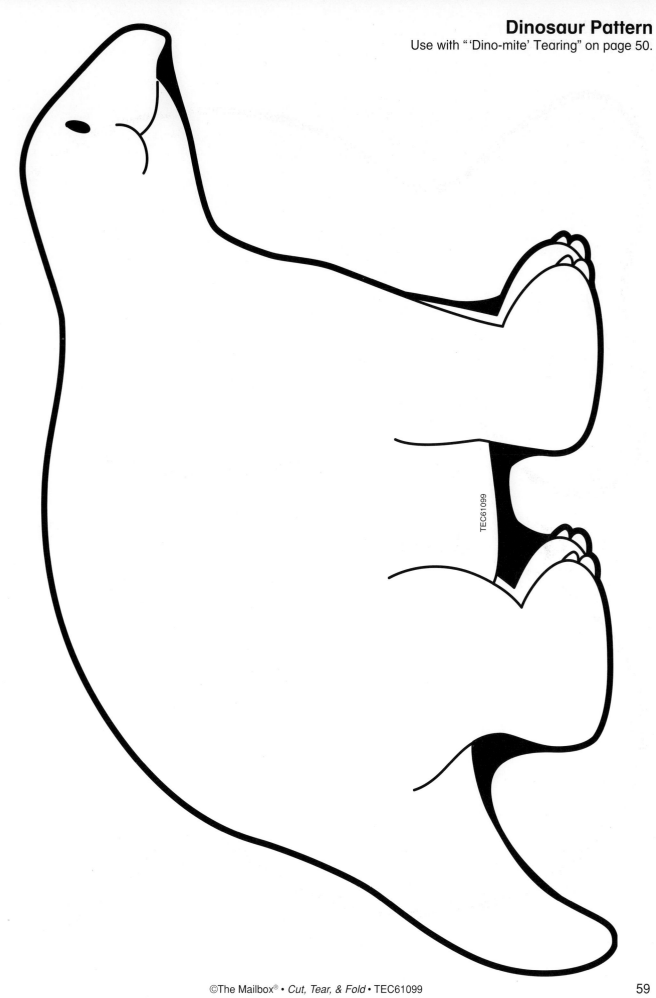

TEC61099

Beach Ball Pattern
Use with "Beach Ball Bonanza" on page 50.

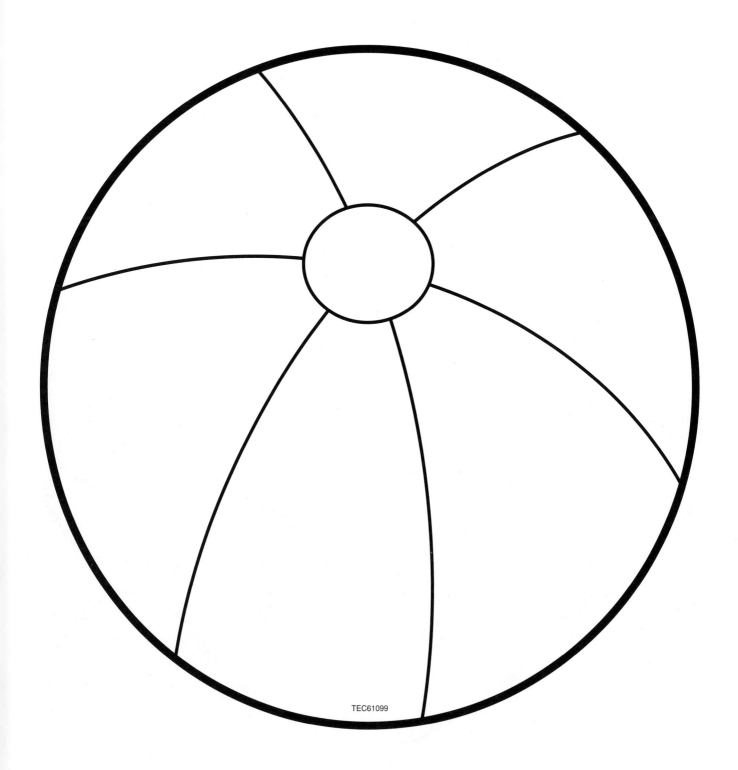

TEC61099

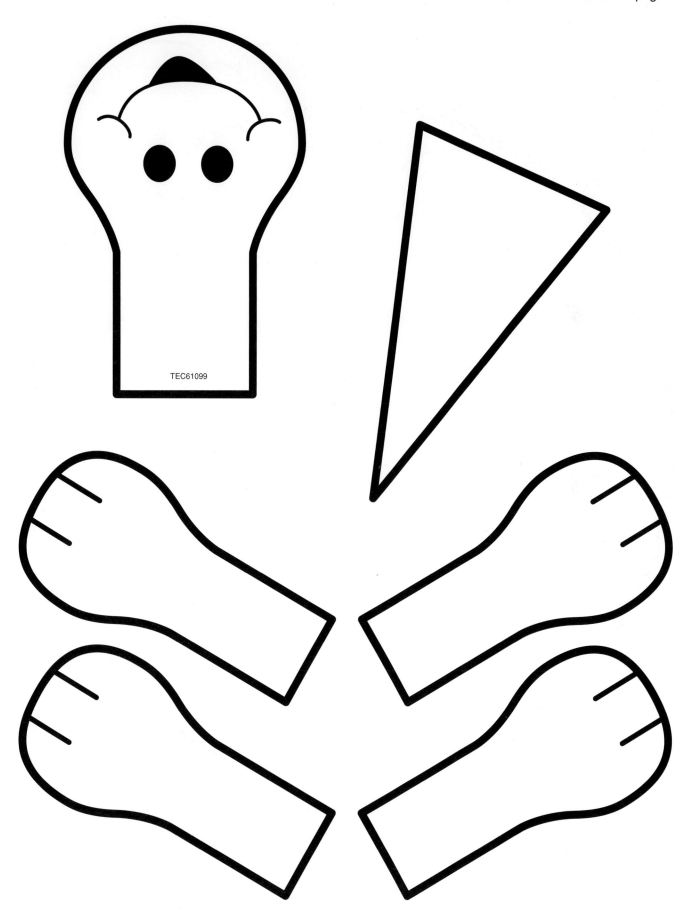

TEC61099

Drip, Drop

Tear.

Glue.

Note to the teacher: Have students tear blue paper to create raindrops.

Name _____

Mud Bath

Color.

Tear.

Glue.

Note to the teacher: Have students tear brown paper to create mud spots on the big pig.

Hiding Out

 Tear.

 Fold.

 Color.

Name _____

Pretty Petals

Tear.

Glue.

©The Mailbox® • *Cut, Tear, & Fold* • TEC61099

Note to the teacher: Have students tear colored paper to create petals.

FOLD

Colorful Creases

A child creates a one-of-a-kind masterpiece by folding his paper in different directions as many times as he likes. When he is satisfied with his creation, he unfolds the paper and uses crayons to trace over each resulting crease.

Materials
- white paper
- crayons

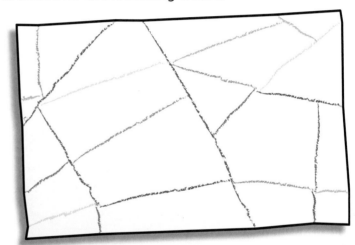

Pet Puppets

Materials
- construction paper —9" square of white
- scissors
- crayons
- tape
- 2 craft sticks

To make two animal puppets, a student folds the square corner to corner. Then she cuts along the crease to make two identical triangles. She folds the corners of the long side of one triangle down to make a puppy and the corners of the other triangle up to make a kitten. She uses crayons to add facial features to each animal. Finally, she tapes a craft stick to the back of each critter.

Center

Invite little ones to wrap a present at this center. A child chooses a box or block and an appropriate-size piece of paper. She folds the paper around the item and tapes it in place. When she is finished, she gives the pretend present to a friend to unwrap.

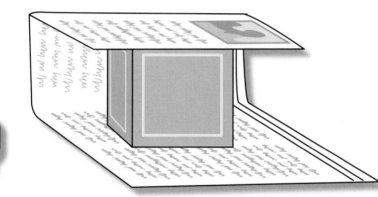

Materials
- small cardboard boxes
- wooden blocks
- wrapping paper, newsprint, or bulletin board paper cut to fit boxes and blocks
- tape

Individual

Shy Bat

To make a bat, a little one folds the top point of the triangle down about halfway. Then she folds each of the two side points in as shown. She adds hole reinforcer eyes and glues ears cut from the scraps to the bat.

Materials
- construction paper
  —triangle of black
  —scraps of black
- 2 hole reinforcers
- scissors
- glue

Lots of Laundry

Invite youngsters to engage in some good, clean fun at this center! Place the laundry basket and a pile of unfolded washcloths at a center. A little one pretends to be doing laundry and "washes" the washcloths. Then she folds each washcloth in fourths and stacks it neatly inside the basket. Laundry's done!

Materials
- laundry basket
- colorful washcloths

Wonderful Wallet

Materials
- wallet cutout (pattern on page 76)
- glue
- pencil
- crayons

To make a wallet, a youngster folds in the two shorter sides of the cutout. Then he folds the cutout in half lengthwise and glues the sides closed as shown. He folds the resulting rectangle in half to resemble a wallet. After helping him add his name, invite him to decorate his wallet as desired.

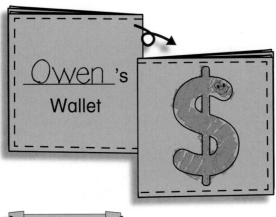

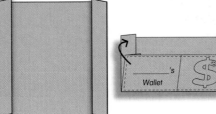

FOLD

Individual — Cozy Cottage

To create a cottage, a child folds the construction paper sheet in half and trims the top corners as shown. He folds the large rectangle to make a door and the remaining rectangles to make windows and glues them to the house. He uses crayons to add desired details to the outside of his house. Then he opens the sheet up and draws himself inside.

Materials
- construction paper
  —9" x 12" sheet
  —4" x 3¾" rectangle
  —two 3½" x 1¾" rectangles
- scissors
- glue
- crayons

Center — A Curly Collage

Youngsters practice their wrapping and curling skills at this center. To begin, attach the bulletin board paper to a wall within student reach. Each child visits the center and wraps a strip around a pencil. Then he glues the curled strip to the bulletin board paper as desired. Invite him to add as many strips as time allows.

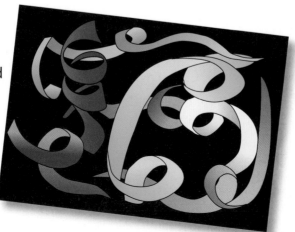

Materials
- construction paper
  —strips of various colors and sizes
- bulletin board paper
- pencils
- glue

Sparkly Snowflake

Individual

To make a snowflake, a child folds a coffee filter in half three times. She cuts notches in the filter and then unfolds it. She removes the backing from the Con-Tact covering and places the covering sticky-side up on a table (with assistance). She sprinkles glitter on the Con-Tact covering and positions her snowflake in the center. Then she sticks the Con-Tact covering to the construction paper (with assistance).

Materials

- construction paper —9" x 12" sheet
- clear Con-Tact covering —8½" square
- coffee filter
- scissors
- glitter

Folding Play Dough

Center

Give youngsters some hands-on experience with color mixing at this center. A child flattens a small amount each of blue and yellow play dough. He places one color atop the other and then presses them together. He folds the play dough mixture over, presses down, and flattens it again to mix the two colors. He continues folding, pressing, and flattening in this manner until the mixture turns green.

Materials

- blue and yellow play dough

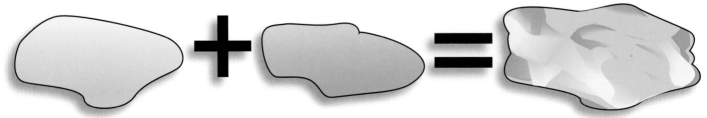

FOLD

Center — Mail Call

The mail youngsters create at this center is extra special—the letters are folded three times! Stack the paper and the envelopes at a center. A youngster writes a letter or draws a picture on one of each size of paper. Then she folds the papers at least three times each and places them inside the corresponding envelopes. If desired, invite her to give her letters to the chosen recipient(s).

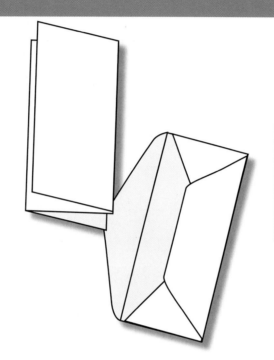

Materials
- sheets and half sheets of copy paper
- business-size and letter-size envelopes
- crayons
- pencil

Individual — Lily Pad Leaper

To make a leaping frog, a child accordion-folds his paper strip and glues one end to his lily pad. Then he glues his frog to the other end of the paper strip. If desired, display the completed projects in a large pond cutout with a title such as "Lots of Leapers."

Materials
- green frog cutout (patterns on page 77)
- construction paper
  —lily pad cut from green
  —strip of green
- glue

A Dandy Duck

To make a duck headband, a child folds the point of the heart up and then partway down as shown. She colors the resulting shape so that it resembles a duck's face and then glues it to the center of the sentence strip. To complete the project, staple the ends of the strip so that it fits the child's head.

Materials
- yellow paper heart
- crayons
- glue
- sentence strip
- stapler

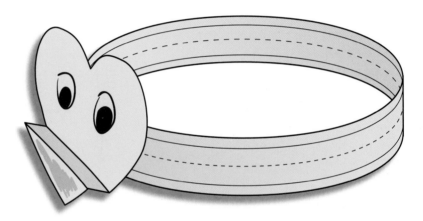

Wiggling Worms

A youngster accordion-folds each worm so that it appears to be moving. After gluing the ends of each worm to his paper, he adds crayon details, such as grass or flowers, to complete the scene.

Materials
- 3 colorful worm cutouts (patterns on page 78)
- construction paper —9" x 12" sheet of white
- glue
- crayons

FOLD

Individual　　Folded Flyer

To make an insect, a child colors the insect body as desired. Next, she accordion-folds the construction paper and pinches it together in the middle to make wings. Staple the middle to secure the folds. Then tape the wings to the back of the body.

Materials
- insect body cutout (patterns on page 79)
- construction paper —9" x 12" sheet
- crayons
- stapler
- tape

Individual　　Beautiful Blossom

To make a flower, a child folds the coffee filter in half twice. She dips portions of the folded filter into various colors of diluted food coloring. After the folded filter dries, she fringe-cuts the top. Next, she opens the filter and folds each tab down to make petals. Then she tapes the resulting flower blossom and the leaf cutouts to the straw.

Materials
- 2 green leaf cutouts
- cone-shaped coffee filter
- bowls of diluted food coloring
- scissors
- straw
- tape

73

Tall Tulips

To make a tulip, a student positions a triangle as shown. She folds the two lower corners upward and glues them in place. She repeats this process for the remaining triangles. Then she glues the tulips to the light blue paper and uses crayons to add desired details.

Materials
- construction paper
  —3 colorful 6" x 4" x 4" triangles
  —9" x 12" sheet of light blue
- glue
- crayons

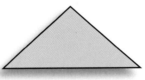

Bustling Boutique

Materials
- doll clothes
- toy cash register
- paper shopping bags
- sheets of tissue paper

Set up this partner center as a clothing store and invite youngsters to go shopping. To prepare, lay out the doll clothes and place the shopping bags and tissue paper near the cash register. Have one student be the cashier and the other be the shopper. After the shopper has selected an item of clothing, he brings it to the cashier. The cashier folds the clothing and then folds tissue paper around it. She unfolds a bag and places the item inside. Then the youngsters return the items to their original locations and switch roles.

FOLD

Individual

Cute Crab

To make a crab, a child accordion-folds the construction paper strips and glues them to the circle, as shown, to make legs. Then he uses his crayons to add eyes and a mouth. Finally, he folds the end of each pipe cleaner half to make pinchers and tapes them to the circle (with assistance).

Materials
- construction paper
  —7" circle of red
  —eight 1" x 6" strips of red
- glue
- red pipe cleaner
  (cut in half)
- tape
- crayons

Individual

Fantastic Sailboat

To make a sailboat, a youngster glues the boat cutout to the blue paper. Next, he accordion-folds the square and pinches one end to make a fan. Staple the fan to secure it and then have the child glue the fan to the boat, as shown, to make a sail. When the glue is dry, he adds additional details if desired.

Materials
- brown sailboat cutout
  (pattern on page 80)
- construction paper
  —9" x 12" sheet of blue
  —6" square
- glue
- stapler

Wallet Pattern

Use with "Wonderful Wallet" on page 68.

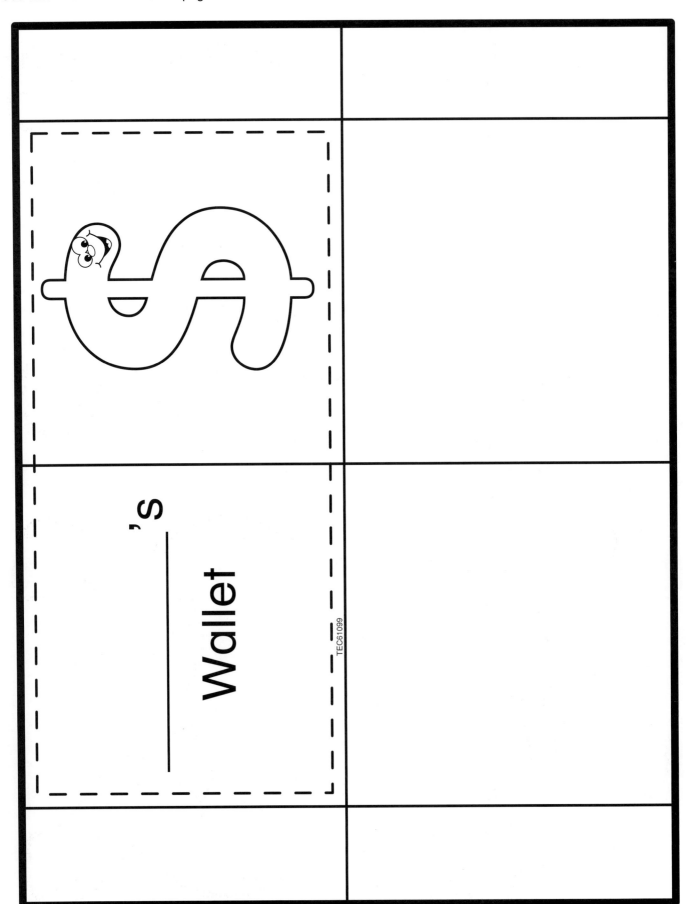

Worm Patterns

Use with "Wiggling Worms" on page 72.

TEC61099

TEC61099

TEC61099

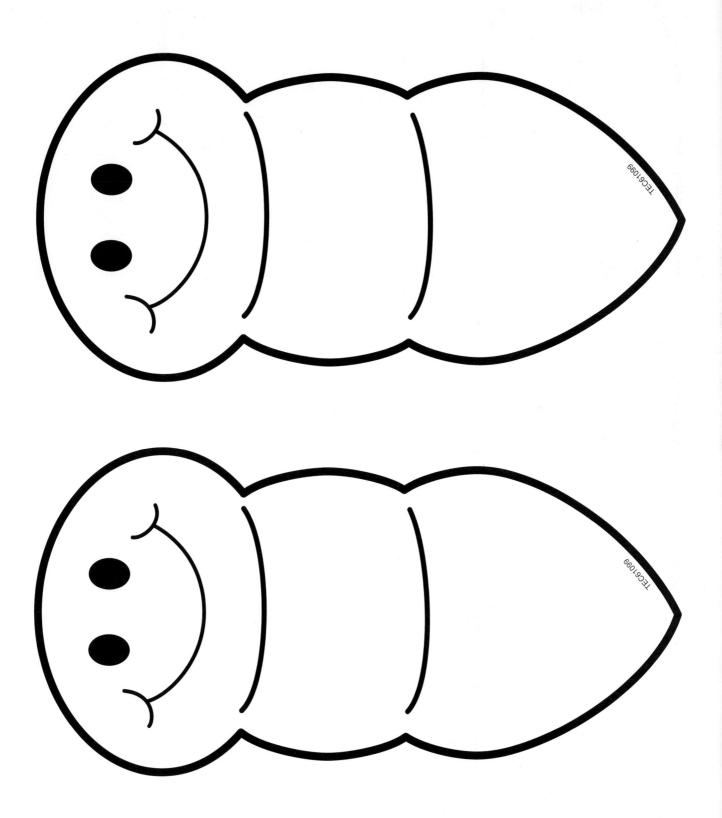

Sailboat Pattern
Use with "Fantastic Sailboat" on page 75.

TEC61099